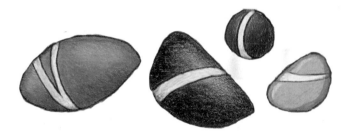

A Handful of Quiet

Happiness in Four Pebbles

Thich Nhat Hanh

PLUM BLOSSOM
BOOKS

BERKELEY, CALIFORNIA

Plum Blossom Books
P.O. Box 7355
Berkeley, California 94707
www.parallax.org

Plum Blossom Books is an imprint of
Parallax Press, the publishing division
of Plum Village Community of Engaged
Buddhism, Inc

Edited by Rachel Neumann
All drawings by Wietske Vriezen
Cover and text design by Debbie Berne

Library of Congress
Cataloging-in-Publication Data

Nhat Hanh, Thich.
 A handful of quiet : happiness in four
pebbles / Thich Nhat Hanh.
   p. cm.
 ISBN 978-1-937006-21-1
 1. Meditation—Buddhism. I. Title.
 BQ5612.N473 2012
 294.3'4435—dc23
                    2012023034

7 8 9 / 19 18 17

CONTENTS

INTRODUCTION

Some years ago, I held a retreat for children in Santa Barbara, California. Many hundreds of children came for the retreat, and their parents came to support them. During that retreat, we invented this pebble practice as a tangible way for children and families to return to their breathing and their bodies and connect with the world around them.

The pebble practice is very simple. It is a little meditation you can do anywhere or anytime. To meditate is to think quietly about something. You may practice pebble meditation at the foot of a tree, in your living room, or wherever you like, but the place should be quiet.

If you have a small bell, that can be very helpful. If not, you might want to use a timer or a stopwatch, or you can do it without any of those things. You can do this practice by yourself, but it is also wonderful to do with your family, with some friends, or with a teacher.

FLOWER, MOUNTAIN, WATER, SPACE

For this meditation, each of the pebbles represents a different image in nature.

a flower

a mountain

calm water

space

Each image—flower, mountain, water, space—embodies a particular quality. After practicing pebble meditation this way, you might find other qualities that you want each pebble to represent. You may want to say that the pebbles represent love, compassion, joy, and inclusiveness, the four qualities of true love. The pebbles could also represent loved ones, such as a mother, father, sibling, close friend, or grandparent. Holding each pebble, we can send our love to that person as we breathe three times.

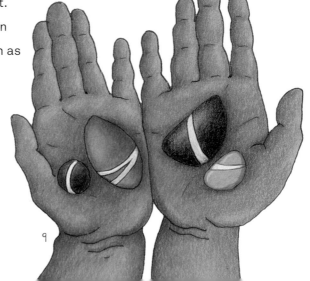

9

FLOWER

When I look at a child, I always see him or her as a flower: fresh, beautiful, and open to the moment. This pebble practice can help preserve our freshness.

When we say, "Breathing in, I see myself as a flower," we don't have to imagine. Each of us is born as a flower, and the seed of flowerness is still in us. If after the practice you can smile easily and feel fresh as a flower, then you are doing the practice correctly.

MOUNTAIN

The second pebble represents a mountain. There is a mountain inside each of us and it keeps us solid and calm. Solidity makes it possible for us to be happy. When you are solid, people can rely on you. When your loved one is solid, you can rely on her. Your solidity is something that you can offer to the person you love.

WATER

The third pebble represents calm water. If you have seen the surface of a lake when it's very still, you may have noticed that it reflects the mountains, clouds, and trees around it perfectly. You can take a picture of the lake, and it is as if you are taking a picture of the surrounding sky, trees, and mountains because they're so clearly reflected in the surface of the lake.

When you are calm, when you are still, you see things as they truly are. You don't distort things. When you are not calm, it's easy to get confused and angry. All of us make a lot of mistakes and create a lot of suffering when we are not calm. Each human being should have enough tranquility to be truly happy. With the third pebble, we cultivate stillness and calm.

SPACE

The last pebble represents space and freedom. Space is freedom, and freedom is the foundation of true happiness. Without freedom, our happiness is not complete. We want to be free from fear, anger, despair, and worries. Breathing in, you can bring a lot of space into yourself. Breathing out, you can bring a lot of space to your beloved ones.

If you love someone, try to offer him more space within and around him, and he will be happy. If you learn flower arranging, you will learn that each flower needs space around it to show its beauty. Human beings are also like this. All of us need some space inside and around us to be truly happy. If we love someone, we should offer our loved one enough space, inside and outside.

If you don't have enough space for yourself, how can you offer space to the person you love? It's important to know how to cultivate more space for ourselves.

Pebble meditation can help children and adults cultivate more freshness, solidity, stillness, and freedom. It can be done anywhere, with pleasure and without difficulty.

DRAWING MEDITATION

Begin by drawing the four objects that your pebbles represent. You can draw with whatever paper and pens, pencils, or crayons you have available.

First draw a flower, any kind of flower. As you draw the flower, notice that you are breathing in and breathing out. Enjoy your in-breath and your out-breath as you draw.

FLOWER A flower represents our freshness. We all have the ability to look at things with fresh eyes and see them as if seeing them for the first time. If we have lost our freshness, all we have to do is practice breathing in and out to restore it. You too are a flower. You have your flowerness. We become light and joyous every time we restore our flowerness.

MOUNTAIN The second thing I would like you to draw is a mountain. Breathe in and out and smile as you draw the mountain. It doesn't have to be a large mountain. It may be snowy or sunny, full of rocks or covered in grass. Maybe you only need two lines in order to make a mountain.

A mountain represents solidity and stability. There is a mountain within you. When you practice sitting and walking with awareness, you grow your capacity to be solid and stable. Solidity and stability are very important for our happiness. They are the mountain within us.

WATER The third thing I would like you to draw is a picture of water. This could be water that you are familiar with and love, perhaps a lake, a pool, a puddle, or a slow-moving river. Choose water that doesn't move too fast, water that can reflect the sky, the clouds, and the mountains. Breathe in and out and smile as you draw the water.

Calm water is beautiful. When water is still, it reflects nature as it really is. When we learn how to mindfully breathe in and breathe out, we are like the still water. We make ourselves still and calm. We can breathe in and out and become calm and serene. Then we can see things as they really are and not get caught in fear, blame, or anger. We have the capacity for great clarity. That is the still water within us.

SPACE The fourth thing I would like you to draw is space. How can you draw space? Make it up! I know you can. You might like to draw the sky, an open field, or a flying bird. Breathe in and out as you draw space. Smile as you draw.

We need to have space in us to be happy. Having enough space helps us experience freedom and joy. Without space we cannot be happy or peaceful. When we look at a table, we may think it is made only of wood. But scientists tell us that the table is made mostly of space. It's hard to believe! But the amount of wood in a table is actually very small.

Our body and consciousness are also like this. We may think we are only made of our bones, organs, blood, and muscles, but if we look closely we also see that we are made of our consciousness, emotions, and many other things. Breathing in and out, we recognize that there is a lot of space within us. To feel free, we need to have space, and so do our loved ones. When we practice in a way that cultivates calm space inside of us, we become free and happy.

We practice in order to restore the flower within.
We practice in order to restore the mountain within.
We practice in order to restore still water within.
We practice in order to restore space within.

PEBBLE MEDITATION

After you have drawn the four images, it's time to find four pebbles. Where can you find them? A beach has a lot of pebbles. So does a mountain. You may even be able to find them on the sidewalk or in the backyard. If you really can't find any, don't worry. You can use four marbles. If you can't find anything else, you can always use four beans until you can find pebbles. Once you have the pebbles, keep them safe in a special bag. That way, you will have them for next time.

You might want to do the next part with a friend or someone in your family. If you are with friends, you may like to invite one or two adults to join you in pebble meditation. Everyone will need their own four pebbles. Sit in a circle. In the center you might want to put a flower. After bowing to the flower, sit beautifully in the lotus position (with legs crossed and both feet resting on opposite thighs), in the half-lotus position (with just one foot on the opposite thigh), simply cross-legged, or in whatever position you like. What is important is that you find a position that is comfortable for you.

Put the four pebbles next to you on your left. Pick up one of the pebbles and place it in the palm of your hand. Look at it with your fresh eyes: the pebble represents a flower. Rest one hand over the hand that holds the pebble. Say to yourself:

Breathing in, I see myself as a flower.
Breathing out, I feel fresh.
Flower, Fresh.

Silently recite the keywords "Flower, Fresh" to yourself as you breathe in and out three times. Each time you recite them, you restore the flower inside of you, and you become fresh. Really see yourself as a flower. We human beings are a kind of flower in the garden of humanity. Every one of us is a flower. Each of us can be a beautiful, fresh, pleasant, and lovable human being. When we have this freshness and beauty, we have a lot to offer to other people and to the world.

After three breaths, look at your pebble, smile to it, and put it down beside you on the floor, on the ground, or on its special place on the page.

you can place a pebble here

Now pick up the SECOND PEBBLE and look at it. This pebble represents a mountain. Put it in the palm of your hand, then place the other hand over it. Now begin to practice with the second pebble:

Breathing in, I see myself as a mountain.
Breathing out, I feel solid.
Mountain, Solid.

Silently recite the key words as you breathe in and out three times. You have a mountain within. You are capable of being solid and stable. After three breaths, put the pebble down on your right.

two pebbles

Pick up the THIRD PEBBLE and look at it. This pebble represents calm water. Put it in the palm of your hand, and place the other hand over it. Begin your practice with the third pebble:

Breathing in, I see myself as still water.
Breathing out, I reflect things as they truly are.
Water, Reflecting.

Recite this silently to yourself as you breathe in and out three times. Still water is within you. You are calm, clear, and serene. Then place the pebble down to your right.

three pebbles

Now pick up the FOURTH PEBBLE. Look at it and smile to it. This pebble represents space. Put it in the palm of your hand, and place the other hand over it. Begin the practice with the fourth pebble:

Breathing in, I see myself as space.
Breathing out, I feel free.
Space, Free.

Recite the keywords silently to yourself as you breathe in and out three times. Space is within you. When we cultivate spaciousness inside and outside of us, we can offer our acceptance and generosity to our beloved ones. Like the moon traveling through the beautiful night sky, we have the capacity for space and freedom no matter where we are. Without freedom, no one can be truly happy. When we touch the space inside of us, we are free. Now place the pebble to your right.

four pebbles

After breathing with the four pebbles, you have completed twelve in-breaths and out-breaths. This ends the pebble meditation. But, if you enjoy it and want to continue, you can move the four pebbles again. When you have finished, place the pebbles back in their bag. If you are with friends, bow to them. If you have a bell with you, invite it to sound as you breathe in and out. Tap the bell lightly once to wake it up, and then a second time, more solidly, to invite a full sound of the bell.

While the bell sounds, breathe in and out three times. If you like, you can smile.

Try it on the next pages . . .

Breathing in, I see myself as a flower.

Breathing out, I feel fresh.

Flower, Fresh.

Breathing in, I see myself as a mountain.

Breathing out, I feel solid.

Mountain, Solid.

Breathing in, I see myself as still water.
Breathing out, I reflect things as they truly are.
Water, Reflecting.

Breathing in, I see myself as space.

Breathing out, I feel free.

Space, Free.

PRACTICE SHEET

Finish the sentences on the following pages to reflect what each pebble means to you.

Underneath each sentence, draw a picture of yourself being that image from nature. You may want to literally draw yourself as a flower, or you can just draw yourself doing something that makes you feel light and fresh as a flower.

FLOWER   FRESH

I feel fresh, energetic, joyful, and playful when

----

you can make your drawing here - - -⤴

MOUNTAIN SOLID

I feel solid, strong, and confident when

WATER REFLECTING

I feel calm, still, and quiet when

SPACE FREE

I feel free, light, and relaxed when

PEBBLE MEDITATION CARDS

Find a quiet spot
Sit in a comfortable position
Sit with your back straight and shoulders relaxed
Notice your in-breath and out-breath
Pick a card
Read slowly so the image sinks in
Close your eyes
Say silently to yourself the keywords IN, OUT
for each in-breath and out-breath
Enjoy the feeling and smile
Take about ten breaths for each card

Breathing in, I see myself as a FLOWER
Breathing out, I feel FRESH

Breathing in, I see myself as a MOUNTAIN
Breathing out, I feel SOLID

Breathing in, I see myself as STILL WATER
Breathing out, I REFLECT things as they are

Breathing in, I see myself as SPACE
Breathing out, I feel FREE

Breathing in, I see myself as a flower,
a human flower
Breathing out, I am beautiful
just as I am and I feel very fresh

IN-BREATH: FLOWER
OUT-BREATH: FRESH

Breathing in, I see myself as
a mountain
Breathing out, I feel solid,
nothing can move or distract me

IN-BREATH: MOUNTAIN
OUT-BREATH: SOLID

Breathing in, I see myself as
still water, a calm, clear lake
in and around me
Breathing out, I reflect things
just as they are,
inside and around me

IN-BREATH: STILL WATER
OUT-BREATH: REFLECTING

Breathing in, I see myself as
the big blue sky, with lots of space
in and around me
Breathing out, I feel very free
and at ease

IN-BREATH: SPACE
OUT-BREATH: FREE

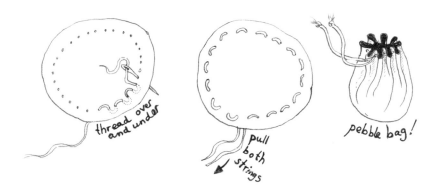

thread over and under

pull both strings

pebble bag!

MAKING A PEBBLE MEDITATION BAG

MATERIALS: yarn, watercolors or fabric paints, markers, ribbons, tapestry needles, children's scissors, buttons, beads, and other decorative items; one 8-inch diameter circle of soft, thin, white or light-colored cloth for each child. (For very young children, it is helpful to cut small holes all around the cloth, one inch from the edge, with about one inch between each hole.)

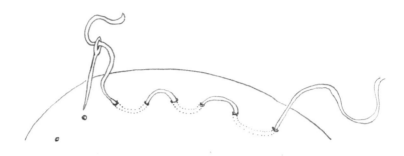

Decorate your cloth circle with the materials you have at hand. If you are using paint or watercolors, allow time for the cloth to dry. When you have finished decorating the cloth, thread the yarn through the holes. An adult can help. When you have woven the yarn all the way around, pull the yarn closed to make a pouch. Each time you finish practicing pebble meditation, put the pebbles into your bag until the next time you practice.

BREATHING IN, BREATHING OUT

Words: Thich Nhat Hanh
Music: Betsy Rose

RESOURCES FOR FAMILY PRACTICE

Related Books from Parallax Press and Plum Blossom Books:

Anh's Anger by Gail Silver

A Basket of Plums by Thich Nhat Hanh

Child's Mind by Christopher Willard

The Coconut Monk by Thich Nhat Hanh

Each Breath a Smile by Sister Susan

The Hermit and the Well by Thich Nhat Hanh

Mindful Movements by Thich Nhat Hanh

A Pebble for Your Pocket by Thich Nhat Hanh

Planting Seeds by Thich Nhat Hanh and the Plum Village Community

Steps and Stones by Gail Silver

The Sun in My Belly by Sister Susan

PRACTICE OPPORTUNITIES WITH CHILDREN

Individuals, families, and young people are invited to practice the art of mindful living in the tradition of Thich Nhat Hanh at retreat communities in France and the United States. For information, please visit www.plumvillage.org or contact:

Plum Village
13 Martineau
33580 Dieulivol, France
www.plumvillage.org

Deer Park Monastery
2499 Melru Lane
Escondido, CA 92026
www.deerparkmonastery.org

Blue Cliff Monastery
3 Mindfulness Road
Pine Bush, NY 12566
www.bluecliffmonastery.org

Magnolia Grove Monastery
123 Towles Rd.
Batesville, MS 38606
www.magnoliagrovemonastery.org

planting seeds of Compassion

If this book was helpful to you, please consider joining the Thich Nhat Hanh Continuation Fund today.

Your monthly gift will help more people discover mindfulness and loving speech, which will reduce suffering in our world.

To join today, make a one-time gift, or learn more, go to: www.ThichNhatHanhFoundation.org.

Or copy the form on the next page and send it to:

Thich Nhat Hanh Continuation
and Legacy Foundation
2499 Melru Lane
Escondido, CA 92026
USA

☐ Yes! I'll support Thich Nhat Hanh's work to increase mindfulness. I'll donate a monthly gift of:

☐ $10   ☐ $30 ($1 a day)   ☐ $50*   ☐ $100   ☐ $ _____ Other

*Your monthly gift of $50 or more earns you a free subscription to
The Mindfulness Bell: a journal of the art of mindful living (US/Canada only).*

☐ Please debit my bank account each month. I've enclosed a blank check marked "VOID."

☐ Please charge my credit card each month.

Your Name(s) _____

Name on Card/Account _____

Credit Card No. _____ Exp. Date _____

www.ThichNhatHanhFoundation.org
info@ThichNhatHanhFoundation.org

**PLUM BLOSSOM
BOOKS**

Plum Blossom Books, the children's imprint of Parallax Press,
publishes books on mindfulness for young people and the grown-ups
in their lives. For a complete list of titles for children, or a free copy
of our catalog, please write us or visit our website.

www.parallax.org

Plum Blossom Books / Parallax Press
P.O. Box 7355
Berkeley, CA 94707